Red Face Stories

Red Face Stories

Compiled by
Frances Coverdale and Clare Price

Front cover illustration by
Bill Tidy

First published in 2006 by

Two Covers, PO Box 780, Richmond, TW10 6TU

Text copyright © Compilation 2006 Frances Coverdale and Clare Price

Front cover illustration copyright © 2006 Bill Tidy

10-digit: ISBN 0-9553782-0-6

13-digit: ISBN 978-0-9553782-0-1

Designed by Christopher Steel

Printed and bound in Great Britain by Biddles Ltd, King's Lynn, Norfolk.

Contents

1 Introduction

4 Matthew William Aston

6 About CHASE

9 Honestly...!

29 Body Bits

51 A Case of Mistaken Identity

69 School Stories

89 Quiet Please!

101 The Things They Say

117 Mothers (Some Children Do Have 'Em)

131 A Final Thought

Illustrators

10 Kitty Wass

30 Bill Tidy

52 Sarah-Jane Gillespie

70 Nick Whitmore

90 Peter James Field

102 Daryl Stevenson

118 Judith Brenner

Stories from...

13	Helen Lederer	77	Linda Duberley
15/57	Kirsty Lang	78/103	Daryl Stevenson
20	Huw Edwards	80	Bel Mooney
24	Mark Austin	83	Gerald Scarfe
33	Jenni Murray	91	Jon Snow
38	Jonny Gould	94	Fiona Bruce
46/109	Ian Wallace	107	John Stapleton
48	Mary Ann Sieghart	122	Sue Cook
56	Phillip Schofield	131	Dilly Keane
61	Maureen Carter		
66	James Gibson		
68/92	Julia Langdon		
72	Keith Chegwin		

...and from

Introduction

The idea for Red Face Stories emerged during a conversation with my sister Clare about how embarrassing my teenage children find me. Probably most children above a certain age are embarrassed by their parents. But as we soon discovered, it's the things children say or do, before they have any concept of embarrassment, that provide the funniest anecdotes. So our original idea was quickly revised, and 'embarrassing mothers' became only a small section of the book.

We're deeply indebted to all the celebrities who rose to the challenge – rather bravely in a couple of cases. We thoroughly enjoyed reading their stories, and it was a good excuse for me to get in touch with former colleagues from my days as a BBC reporter and newsreader.

We're incredibly grateful to our illustrators, none of whom have charged for their work. Bill Tidy responded to my request for 'an' illustration, and when his cartoon on page 30 arrived in the post a few days later, I was so encouraged that I cheekily asked him to do the front cover as well. Amazingly he agreed - even allowing us to auction the original at our fund-raising Ball.

At the outset, we promised anonymity to all but the celebrity contributors. Most of their names are listed alphabetically, and we leave it to them to decide whether to admit which story is theirs. Some contributors remain unnamed, including several who responded to my request on the BBC Word of Mouth message board and whose real identities I don't even know.

Family members, friends and acquaintances have entered into the spirit of the book with real enthusiasm and helped in a variety of ways. Our particular thanks go to Simon Dinnick, Philippa Stancomb, Martin Evans, Mary Rose Rivett-Carnac, Daryl Stevenson and Vivienne Mather. Also to Nicky Rennie from CHASE Head Office, who persuaded several of her celebrity contacts to give us their anecdotes.

We're especially grateful to Chris Steel, who was invited to design the book (without payment) and did so willingly, even though it entailed far more work than any of us had envisaged. Thanks also to Matt Spencer for his assistance.

Finally, our heartfelt thanks to Tina Aston. Her eight-year-old son Matthew was the first child to die at Christopher's, and her decision to pay for the printing from the Matthew Aston Memorial Fund means that all the proceeds from the book will go to CHASE.

We hope you'll enjoy the Red Face Stories - and if they jog any memories of your own, do please email us at redface@covermail.co.uk and we'll consider a follow-up.

Frances Coverdale

Dedicated to
Matthew William Aston 26.7.93 – 5.1.02

How do I find the words to describe how wonderful
Matthew was? Where do I begin? With his eyes, his smile, his
love? He was so caring. You can see from his poem the kind
of child he was. He touched the hearts of everyone he met.

Tina Aston

I have a dream that people look after each other

I have a dream that people do not hurt animals

I have a dream that people are not horrible

I have a dream that there will be peace all over the world

I have a dream that people do not bully

I have a dream that people help the poor

I have a dream that people do not fight

I have a dream that people will get better

I have a dream that all the people in the world have a good life

Matthew Aston, aged 8

About CHASE

It was Boxing Day 2001. Eight-year-old Matthew Aston had spent Christmas at home but his condition was deteriorating fast and his parents, Tina and Graham, knew they could no longer cope.

Matthew had been diagnosed with a brain tumour less than nine months earlier. He was being treated at the Royal Marsden Hospital and had had a major operation at Great Ormond Street. When their doctor suggested referring him to a children's hospice that had opened just the previous month, Tina was full of dread.

"We didn't realise what a children's hospice was," Tina says. "But as soon as we walked through the door of Christopher's, we knew it was right. It was such a lovely place - happiness, sadness and caring all rolled into one."

Christopher's is run by CHASE Hospice Care for Children, which provides a service to the families of life-limited children and teenagers from South West London, Surrey and Sussex. The nine-bedroom hospice near Guildford offers specialist respite, palliative and end of life care, while the

CHASE Community Care Team provides the same care and support to the families in their own homes.

As Tina discovered, the emphasis at CHASE is very much on the family as a whole. "We all moved in - my parents, sister and brother too, right up until Matthew's funeral. They looked after all of us in the family rooms upstairs and they couldn't have been more supportive."

During Matthew's last ten days, two nurses were dedicated to his care. "They were there for us when we needed them, but they didn't just take over. We were able to care for him too. They treated us with such sensitivity."

Matthew was a big Chelsea fan and had told Bridget Turner, the Director of Care, that his hero was Gianfranco Zola. She secretly arranged for Zola to come and visit Matthew, two days before he died.

"Matthew was very poorly, but he recognised Zola immediately and his face just lit up," Tina says. Zola publicly dedicated his next goal to Matthew.

Since the Community Care Team started its work in June 1999, CHASE has helped the families of more than 500 children and young people with a wide range of conditions, including genetic and metabolic disorders, major organ failure, cancer and neurologically acquired conditions. It is currently supporting almost 300 families.

The service is free to the families, but expensive to run. To keep going, CHASE has to raise £3.2m every year - almost all of it from charitable donations. To find out more, visit the website at www.chasecare.org.uk.

Honestly...!

© Kitty Wass 2006

As a child my mother sent me to the Co-op, clutching a purse with the money and a shopping list. I entered the grocery section and was immediately approached by 'Fat Bob'.

"Well, son, what do you want?" he asked jovially.

"My Mum said not to get you, because you cheat on the change," I innocently replied.

I was shopping at Debenhams in Edinburgh with my three-year-old daughter, and had very little time left on the meter. Seeing the queue at the till, I knew my time was up, so I made my way over to pay, asking Genevieve to come with me.

She wandered over to a rail of pink corduroy trousers. I was getting agitated and called again for her to come over. I couldn't leave my place in the queue. I saw her putting her finger up her nose and digging hard. I shouted at her to come over because we needed to go and it was my turn to be served.

She walked up to me; I paid for my things and handed her a paper hankie - which she declined, saying: "It's OK, Mummy. I wiped it on those pink trousers over there."

I was given a beautiful birthday cake by a friend who could not attend my party. It was delivered by a caterer and had all manner of stars and sparklers and amazing artefacts. I was very impressed and put it high on the bookshelf out of harm's way, while my daughter (then aged seven) and I duly admired it.

The party came and went, but I had a few drinks too many and completely forgot to cut and serve the personalised cake.

The following week my daughter and I met up with my friend, who asked me how I had enjoyed the cake at my party. I panicked and was well into an elaborate spiel about how much I loved the cake and how the guests were enthralled by the design and the glorious taste, when my daughter piped up: "But Mummy, it's still on the bookshelf where you left it."

Helen Lederer, comedienne

Our daughter, aged four, answered the phone to her nanny's new boyfriend. Having established that the nanny was out, he wanted to leave a message with someone more reliable than a child, so he asked: "Is your Mummy or Daddy there?"

"Yes," she replied helpfully. "Mummy's here in the kitchen and Daddy's doing a poo."

I was with my six-year-old son walking down a street in our area, when a woman in a huge SUV/Landrover stopped to ask me for directions. Just as I finished speaking to her, my son piped up in a loud voice: "Mum why were you so nice to that lady? You hate people who drive those big cars!"

Kirsty Lang, presenter Front Row, Radio 4

We'd moved to Nairobi with our young son and were keen to make new friends. One woman was particularly well connected among the expat community and, on the advice of somebody else I had met, I asked her to tea.

She was charm itself, but for some reason, Hugo would not take his eyes off her. It was clearly making her feel uncomfortable and finally she asked him why he was staring.

He piped up: "Well I can only see one face. Mummy was told you had two."

My husband had been talking about a neighbour and described her as a 'two faced old so-and-so'. It didn't occur to him that our son, who was five or six at the time, would take him literally. Or that the neighbour might be present at a party we were attending later.

There was stunned silence when Luke said: "Dad, Mrs (.....) hasn't got two faces!"

It just shows that you can't be too careful what you say within earshot of small children.

Some French friends were deep in conversation with a family they were visiting when, for no apparent reason, their young son asked to see the hand of their host.

The man offered it for scrutiny and the little boy carried out his examination, after which he exclaimed with much surprise: "Mais non, Papa, tu avais tort - il n'a PAS de poil dans la main."

Literally this means: "No Daddy, you were wrong - he HASN'T got a hair in his hand." 'Avoir un poil dans la main' is an idiomatic expression meaning 'to be extremely lazy'.

I must have been about eight years old. We had a lady guest staying, and for some reason one mealtime the question of housekeeping came up.

As a cocky little boy I had to throw in my pennyworth. "Oh, if I were housekeeping, I should find it easy," I said. "It's just a matter of ordering the right things. Anyway," I added, "I certainly shouldn't have any visitors."

We were viewing yet another house in our protracted attempts to move home. I had my five children in tow (not recommended for these duties). The house had clearly had a new cream carpet laid, on which I soon noticed a trail of brown sludge behind us. I tried to swipe some lumps of mud away when the estate agent's back was turned. This made things much worse.

She started looking at me in a curious way. "I say!" she squeaked, "are you... erm... Michael... erm... Martyn... erm... that newsreader?" "Yes," I said, breaking my first rule, which is to deny everything. "You look so much younger off the telly." "Ah," I said, "that's very kind of you." This was a mistake because it encouraged her. "Do you mind me asking how old you are?" Stupidly, I told her I was 39.

Within a micro-second, Sammy (then seven years old)

had piped up: "Daddy's telling lies. He's 42. He always says he's 39 but he's 42. Mummy's 39. He's 42 and he'll be 43 on his next birthday."

I wanted to throttle Sammy. I shoved him down some steps into a bathroom and made vicious threatening noises. He looked on with irritating superiority and said: "It's wrong to tell lies - you always say that to me."

I made a hasty exit, past the trail of dried mud, ignoring the estate agent's questions, and straight to the car. We didn't buy the house.

Huw Edwards, BBC News presenter

I was working at a delicatessen, where we'd sell off end-cuts of ham, bacon and other meats at less than half price. One day, a smart looking woman came into the shop with a little boy and asked for quite a quantity of these meats, adding: "It's for the dog."

Her son looked puzzled for a moment, then said: "But Mummy, we haven't got a dog."

I was on a bus with my very young son, and asked for one ticket. The conductor asked my little boy: "How old are you sonny?" Little boy's reply: "I'm only three on the buses!"

We were having trouble with the builders. The job was taking forever and the bill was increasing by the day. We made the mistake of talking about it over breakfast within earshot of an eight-year-old daughter, who didn't seem to be taking much notice.

My wife was being very rude about the builders and I was agreeing with her. But the anger passed, and we decided to give the builders another week before confronting them about the worm-like pace of the work.

Half an hour later the doorbell rang and, as always, our daughter rushed to answer it. It was the builder - and before we could get to the door, she was telling him how awful we thought he was.

"Mum and Dad think you're being really slow and lazy and they're really cross.

They might not pay you unless you start doing the
work properly."

All absolutely true of course - but red faces for us and
the builder. They did get the job done pretty quickly
after that though.

Mark Austin, ITV News presenter

I was walking down the road with my four-year-old daughter when we saw coming towards us a particularly boring neighbour, well-known locally for telling long-winded stories with no punchline.

I felt myself grind to a halt as my daughter said in a clear piping voice: "Mummy, is this the lady you said was so boring?" I managed to keep my voice even and laughed and said: "No, of course not," and the neighbour laughed as well, doubtless with relief. It then became impossible to move away as she chattered to me brightly, on and on, searching my face, presumably for signs that I'd been lying.

From that day I could feel a frozen smile coming on if she caught my eye. Thankfully she moved house soon after, but the memory of it still gives me the shivers.

I have difficulty remembering names and this always causes embarrassment when it comes to introductions, so long ago I adopted the technique of doing only half the introduction.

When I was working at the University of Ibadan in Nigeria, I took my 17-year-old son to a Christmas drinks party attended by a lot of my colleagues. I found I needed to use my favoured technique when confronted with a colleague, a historian whom I knew very well, but whose name escaped me at that particular moment.

"Oh," I said to him, "meet my son Jonathan." They duly shook hands. In the ensuing silence, Jonathan said to me, loud and clear: "What did you say the gentleman's name was?"

When I was two, and not yet potty trained, my Mum took me swimming - and was horrified when she spotted something nasty floating up from my trunks.

Too embarrassed to admit that her son was the perpetrator of a deed that would inevitably lead to chaos and revulsion, she whisked me out of the water and told me she was taking me to the loo. To which I shouted: "But I don't need to go - I've already done it in the pool!"

Body Bits

© Bill Tidy 2006

We were at the local DIY store with our daughter, who was then about two years old. Suddenly we realised that we couldn't find her, and began to panic.

An assistant came along and told us where to look: in the window, where there was a bathroom display.

She was using the toilet!

We took the potty with us wherever we went. One day on the top floor of Marks & Spencer, while browsing through shirts in the men's department, I realised that my eldest son had climbed out of the pushchair, whipped out the potty and done his 'business' before I could do anything about it.

Covering the vessel with a discreet tissue, I had to negotiate the tandem pushchair to the lift, ride down in it accompanied by some puzzled shoppers, then make our way out of the shop and find a handy drain. Well, it could have been worse.

My most embarrassing moment ever was on a P&O Ferry from the south coast to France with four-year-old Ed and six-month-old Charlie. We were having lunch in the restaurant when Ed, à propos of absolutely nothing, suddenly piped up: "Mum...?" in the tone that warns you you're in for trouble. "Yes darling, what is it?" "Well, Mum, you know when you and Dad made Charlie - did he put his willy in your mouth or your bottom?"

Children have voices designed to be heard by absolutely everybody. Ah, the dangers of honest and early sex education!

Jenni Murray, Woman's Hour presenter

Our son was about six and was accompanying me on a shopping trip to the supermarket. As we were waiting to be served at the delicatessen counter, he suddenly asked me in a loud voice: "Daddy, you know the juice a man gives a woman to make a baby - what colour is it?"

I could feel fellow customers staring as I replied calmly (and quietly): "Well, it's white." He went silent for a moment, then persisted: "When you say white, what sort of white is it?"

I muttered something about the inside of an After Eight and was greatly relieved when the deli assistant turned to take my order.

When Joseph was six, the business of puberty and the physical changes taking place in his teenage cousin were a source of tremendous interest to him.

One Saturday night we were going out and had booked a new babysitter - a boy of about 17, terribly tall and handsome. Joseph was immediately impressed and full of admiration. For once he was quite quiet.

By way of a 'conversation opener', and presumably as a sort of acknowledgment of knowing what was what with Big Boys, he turned to the babysitter and asked him: "Have you got pubic hair?"

When our children were young I used to belong to a local babysitting circle. One evening I went to babysit for a little boy of five or six. His mother informed me that her son was very excited to have a babysitter called Mary Rose because his class was doing a project on Henry VIII's warship, the *Mary Rose*, at school.

When his parents had left, the boy asked me what it was like to be the *Mary Rose*. I told him that it was cold and wet and that I'd lain on the sea-bottom for hundreds of years. He then asked if they'd found anything interesting on me.

Getting into my stride, I started to list some of the objects, including Tudor arrow heads, cooking tools and also lots of cannon balls. I was slightly taken aback when he exclaimed mischievously: "Yes, I can see two of those."

I used to help out in a Church crèche. One time, I was playing with some toddlers and a father came over to thank me for looking after his daughter.

Just as I was about to reply, one of the little girls in the group decided to pat my chest and say: "Your boobs are very big." I pretended not to have heard her, so she repeated her 'compliment' in a louder voice. The father went bright red and left.

When I married my gorgeous wife Rachel I was lucky enough, not just to become a husband, but also a Dad. A step-dad to be exact - to the Big Guy (Max) and to the Tinks (Jack). The boys were six and four respectively when we got married and both full of mischief and fun.

I'd always wanted to be a Dad, so having a ready-made family at 41 was fab. But Rachel and I also wanted one of our own to complete our family, and thankfully we were blessed with the arrival of little Tommy, 14 months after we had tied the knot.

Three boys is a handful in any language, so as soon as Mum and baby were safely home, I enlisted for the chop. It all happened a lot quicker than expected and was, as predicted, a sensitive time.

On the day in question, Rachel warned Jack and Max that I was in no fit state for our usual rough and tumble, explaining that I'd had an operation that had left me black and blue where the sun don't shine.

Amazingly I felt well enough to go to work the next day, and even volunteered to run the boys to school. It was a decision I was soon to regret, as on arrival Jack spotted his teacher, leapt out of the car and shouted at the top of his voice: "Miss Murray, Miss Murray... Jonny's balls are all black!"

Jonny Gould, Channel 5 Sports presenter

A small friend of ours was on a crowded tube during a weekday rush hour, accompanying her mother en route into town. She was four or five - young enough to have no inhibitions - and was very interested in all the people around her.

Her mother was strap-hanging and Emma was beside her, hanging on for dear life but sizing up the other passengers. Right beside her, also standing, was a moustachioed businessman.

The child beamed up at him. "You look just like my Daddy!" she announced. The man smiled back in a friendly fashion, in the way that adults do to charming small children without, of course, being too friendly or encouraging.

"Thank you," he said. "That's good."

Emma was set on a serious conversation, however.

"My Daddy's got a moustache, just like yours," she said in a piping voice that filled the carriage. The man duly acknowledged that he did, indeed, have a moustache.

"And," said Emma, warming to her theme, "he wears a hat like you do as well." "We must look very alike," the man said politely.

"Ye-es," said Emma, considering this and still speaking to the entire company of commuters. "But have you got a willy, too?"

I used to help look after a little girl and would often take her with me to the local shops. She became quite friendly with the lady at the newsagent, and the two of them would have a chat when we went in.

One Saturday, she went into the shop with her Dad instead. Obviously proud of him and keen to show him off in the best possible light, she went up to the shopkeeper and told her: "This is my Daddy - he's got a big willy."

We have always been very relaxed about nudity in our family and when the children were little, they would come in for a chat when my husband or I were in the bath.

So when my daughter went to stay with a friend, aged about three, she thought it was perfectly natural to walk into the bathroom to brush her teeth, even though her friend's father was in there having a soak.

His wife told us later that on her way to the basin, she had taken a look at his appendage and commented: "My Daddy's is bigger than yours!"

On my gap year, I was a nanny for three children -
Betsy (aged four), Emily (two) and Harry (15 months).

One day when I was changing Harry's nappy, Emily
poked his willy and asked me what it was. I got
flustered and told her I didn't know. She poked it again
and asked why she didn't have one.

Harry wasn't looking fantastically happy at having his
private parts poked and we were in a rush to leave the
house, so I stupidly told her that hers had dropped off,
but that it didn't matter. She looked quite happy with
this explanation and off we went to playgroup.

That afternoon, I saw Emily in the garden searching
under bushes and plants. I asked her what she was
doing and she told me she was looking for her missing
willy. I retracted what I'd said earlier and told her the

truth about why boys had willies and girls didn't, but she didn't believe a word of it and insisted that hers was lost.

I had no option but to explain to her parents why she was obsessed with finding her missing willy. Not one of my finer nannying moments.

Few memories last a lifetime. One of mine goes back to 1925, when I was six. My mother took me with her on a shopping trip to a famous ladies' outfitter in Oxford Street, where one of the assistants led her to the dress department and kept calling her 'Modom'.

The underground journey, my first, was exciting; the shopping was deadly boring. But in those days little boys had to do as they were told - and there was the promise of a lovely tea afterwards.

As we sat down in the café, a large lady approached us and in a ringing baritone cried: "May, what a coincidence. Can I join you?"

"Of course, Cousin Mary. Ian, this is my cousin. Give her a kiss."

I was reluctant. No wonder - Cousin Mary had

a splendid moustache. All through tea, I was saying: "Mummy...?" and my mother, knowing what was on my mind, fended me off, with: "Have another Swiss roll." Then: "Mummy...?" to which she'd answer: "Would you like an éclair?"

The ruse succeeded. We parted company with our hirsute relative without the fatal question being asked. But on the way home I was violently sick in the tube. Modom had a red face all over again.

Ian Wallace OBE, retired singer and actor

We took our then two-year-old daughter, Evie, away for the weekend at a smart country-house hotel which purported to be family-friendly. The other guests were decidedly frosty at having their weekend invaded by a toddler, so we took her to the indoor pool. Even there the other swimmers looked disapprovingly at her every time she opened her mouth.

Worse was to come, though, when she looked at an extremely fat man and said to me: "Mummy, why has that man got bosoms?" "Ssssh," I said. She repeated the question even louder. "I'll tell you later," I hissed.

Undaunted, she walked straight up to him, dripping wet, and said very loudly: "Excuse me, why have you got bosoms?" Shamefaced, he replied: "I suppose I'm just rather fat."

Mary Ann Sieghart, Times columnist

My husband, children and I were having supper with my sister one day, when I noticed that my sister was convulsed with laughter.

When she finally managed to say what was amusing her so much, she told us that she'd seen our 18-month-old daughter put her finger in her nose, produce a fine bogey, and hold it up for my husband's inspection.

He was talking at the time and, assuming that the proffered item was something to eat, took it into his mouth, remaining blissfully unaware of what had happened until my sister was able to explain.

It was the children's school Sports Day, and assorted relatives were assembled beside the make-shift running track, eagerly cheering their young ones on. Among the spectators was the grandmother of one of the little boys. Between races, she walked under the low branch of a tree... and emerged minus her wig.

A Case of
Mistaken Identity

I was working as a doorman at the Copthorne Tara Hotel in Kensington. As is customary at smart London hotels, the job entailed wearing top hat and tails.

I have to admit, I'm quite rotund - and when one little lad arrived with his father, he was sure he recognised me from somewhere. His father, though, was highly embarrassed when the boy pointed to me excitedly and said: "Oh look Daddy, it's the Fat Controller!"

I was on the Tube with my three-year-old daughter. Opposite us was a rather elegant lady dressed head-to-toe in black, with a long black coat, pointed black shoes and long black hair.

Elise stared at the woman, her eyes getting wider and wider. Finally she turned to me, bursting with enthusiasm, and declared in her loudest voice: "Mummy, it's so exciting. There's a real live witch sitting opposite me."

As a spiritual and crystal healer, I gave Mark, a new friend, a tiger's eye crystal as a present. He took it home to his partner and her eight-year-old son.

Louis, the child, was fascinated beyond words and told his friends all about it. When asked where Mark had got it, Louis replied: "From a client at work, who's a magician."

I was the one who caused the embarrassment and the poor victim was the mother of a famous pop star, who was appearing on *This Morning.*

One of the wonderful things about working on the programme is the many and varied people I get to meet, from all walks of life and of all ages - and each and every one of them has a story to tell.

By the time I arrive at the studios, I've already read through the script and worked out the questions I'm going to ask. We all meet up in the Green Room, a good place to break the ice and have a bit of a chat, and even impress the guests by knowing their names.

However it's no place to be smart, as I was when I mistook the pop star's mother for a guest - and asked how her friends had accepted her sex change!

Phillip Schofield, presenter This Morning

I was with my son, who was about four at the time, on a crowded train going down to spend Christmas with family in Somerset. We were sitting at a table opposite a very butch looking lady with cropped hair, when he said in a loud voice, staring straight at her: "Mum is that a man or lady?"

I smiled in an embarrassed way at the woman, who was not looking at all amused, and replied: "A lady darling. Now why don't you play with your soldiers?" But oh no, he wanted to carry on. "She looks like a man with bosoms, Mum."

I grabbed his arm and fled to the buffet car, and didn't return until the woman had got off.

Kirsty Lang, presenter Front Row Radio 4

My father was a surgeon, and grateful patients would send him Christmas gifts. In order not to embarrass Dad, the gift would often be chocolates to us three girls. They would pile up under the Christmas tree.

One school holidays, after Christmas, I was going to stay with a girlfriend in Lincolnshire. Very big house and very rich parents. I needed a gift. Ma immediately suggested that I take one of the many boxes of chocolates. We picked a circular one, still wrapped up, and I duly went to Grimsby.

My first night, after dinner and all of us cosily round the fire, the chocolates were opened with great delight and fanfare, but oh... to my horror, round the edge and individually wrapped in gold paper were the letters spelling Jane, Sally and Gillian.

My father loved to play jokes and would often buy tricks from a magic shop. Once he gave me a lump of sugar and told me to drop it into his coffee. Out came a small floating duck... it was magic! I was so thrilled with this trick that I asked my father to let me bring a sugar lump to school the next day to surprise my teacher (a nun) for her birthday.

During break, all the children gathered around with small presents for the teacher. With her permission, I dropped the sugar lump into her cup. But instead of the little duck I was expecting, a red heart emerged on the surface with the words 'I love you' on it.

It was another of my father's jokes.

I was about 12 and enduring a long and boring car journey with my parents. I was at that age when everything they did irritated me. So when they stopped for a call of nature at a public lavatory, my first thought was how old they were and how weak their bladders. I moodily told them I didn't need to go.

It was only after a minute or so that I realised I did need to. Sheepishly I followed them, ignoring the first flight of stairs, saying 'Gentlemen', and taking the second staircase to what I assumed was the Ladies.

Unfortunately, that too led down to the Gents. I don't know who was more embarrassed - me, my father or the gentleman standing at the next urinal.

Our daughter was born a few days before Christmas. As a special treat for her fifth birthday we organised a trip to the theatre to see Sleeping Beauty, followed by dinner at a favourite Italian restaurant.

When the curtain fell, she was clearly stage-struck and keen to prolong the magic. She acted out various roles on the way to the restaurant, and when we arrived, she wanted us to perform as well. As stage director, she assigned parts. "I'm Sleeping Beauty," she said. "Daddy, you're the handsome prince."

At this point there was one of those lulls in the surrounding conversations, and the crowded dining area fell silent. Indeed, hers was the only audible voice as she pointed to me and said: "And you're the wicked stepmother!"

Maureen Carter, crime writer

I was working as a nanny, looking after two little girls aged two and 15 months. One morning I was with the two-year-old when I noticed a fox in the garden.

"Look! Sophie," I said, "a fox." "Dog," said Sophie.

"No, it's like a dog, but it's called a fox," I corrected. "Dog," said Sophie.

"No, it is very like a dog," I persisted, "but it's called a fox. Can you say fox?" "F**k," said Sophie, trying hard to copy what I'd said.

"NO! Fox. F.O.X. Fox. Say fox." "F**k," said Sophie again, finding my alarm rather funny.

At this point, I concluded it was safest to drop the subject.

Later that day, some neighbours came to the house, bringing their dog with them, a Lassie look-alike. Sophie eyed it keenly, but she was a very shy and reserved child and she was totally silent - until the neighbours were about to leave. Then she started to run round and round the dog pointing at it and shouting: "f**k, f**k, f**k!"

I later confessed to the parents, who found the incident very funny. They told me the neighbours had already phoned them to check that I wasn't some weirdo who specialised in teaching profanities to children.

When my son was about three, he and I were sitting in the doctor's surgery patiently waiting our turn. To keep him amused, we read one of the surgery's children's books. Very politically correct, it showed people of different nationalities in work clothes, asking us to guess what they did.

Being an observant child, my son clearly identified the Chinese man with a stethoscope as a doctor and the Englishman with the milk bottles as a milkman. When he came to the picture of a turbanned Indian man, whose actual occupation I forget, his response was immediate: "He works at the Post Office."

Before the last war, we were on holiday in Whitby. I was about eight, and fortunately a skinny little thing. I was rather full of the joys of being on holiday and having more of my father's company than usual.

He went into a bank to draw some money. I thought I'd give him a surprise and play a joke on him, so I ran up behind him and leapt onto his back. Except that it wasn't *his* back.

In my early years of competing, around the age of seven and eight, I can only describe my actions as a comedy of errors. At my first ever swimming competition, I was in and out of the toilet with nerves so much I missed my race.

The following competition, I arrived late and missed my race again. My team were starting to lose patience with me, but they gave me another chance - going first in a ten-man relay.

This time I made it to the starting block. But then the thought hit me: "What stroke am I supposed to be doing?" I had no idea.

"Take your marks," said the starter. I knew it was either breaststroke or freestyle, I was so bad at backstroke and fly. BANG went the gun.

I thought I'd just copy the boy next to me; that seemed like a good idea. I hit the water and off came the goggles. I couldn't see anything so I decided to go with freestyle.

At this point, my parents sneaked out of the fire escape. I was supposed to be doing breaststroke. The team were instantly disqualified but the other nine guys still had to swim, knowing it was for nothing. I wasn't Mr Popular as you can probably guess.

That was my red faced moment. I hear you say: "At least your trunks didn't come down." My answer: "We'll save that story for another time."

James Gibson MBE, world swimming champion

The day that Nelson Mandela was released from prison had a considerable impact on my four-year-old daughter, who was very affected by the fact that I was watching the TV with tears pouring down my face.

"Why are you crying Mummy?" she asked, worriedly. I explained, in simple words, that I was profoundly moved by the fact that a man who had been unjustly imprisoned for over twenty years was now, at last, being released as a symbol of the end of a bad system of government.

The next day we got on a bus in West London, on which one of the other passengers was a grizzled, elderly black man with greying hair. "Look Mummy! There's Nelson Mandela!" she cried at the top of her voice, pointing at him, delightedly. Everyone on the bus, including Nelson's lookalike, roared with laughter.

Julia Langdon, writer and broadcaster

School Stories

NICHOLAS

Shortly before our younger daughter started at primary school, my husband had a vasectomy. During Olivia's first term, her class put on a special assembly on the theme of babies.

Her form teacher brought in her new baby to show off to all the pupils and teachers, after which some of the children stood up to say something on the subject.

Olivia, in her loudest, clearest voice, told the entire school that she'd love to have a little brother or sister, but she couldn't, because: "Daddy's had the light turned out at his seed factory!"

My daughter Rose was five years old and I took her to see me take part in some filming for Comic Relief's Red Nose Day. We were recording a spoof of the BBC's Casualty, where Phil Collins and I were dressed up as nurses.

I took Rose to school on the Monday morning and, as was the norm, had a laugh and a joke with her teachers. However, things took a turn for the worse when I picked Rose up in the afternoon. Teachers deliberately ignored me; so did other members of staff and some of the Mums. It was very odd - they just weren't as friendly as normal.

I was troubled, as this went on for a whole week. It was only when our stint on Comic Relief was aired that the reason for their blanking became apparent.

Little did I know it, but Rose had gone round the whole school telling everyone how her Daddy and his best friend enjoyed dressing up as nurses, and that over the weekend Daddy and his mate dressed up for her.

She also told everyone how much I enjoyed it and how she thought her Daddy looked nice as a woman and that my lipstick was red, I wore long socks with stretchy strips to hold them up (stockings), but Daddy's dress was very tight. No wonder I was blanked!

Luckily, most people at the school saw my antics on Comic Relief - but even some 12 years later people still take the Mickey.

Keith Chegwin, TV presenter

Our five-year-old daughter was meeting her new teacher and was obviously keen to impress with her general knowledge. Unfortunately she didn't quite get her facts right when she boasted: "I know the name of the Queen... Elizabeth Vagina."

We'd been out for a pub lunch with our two young sons. In the middle of the table were the salt, pepper and mustard, so I decided to teach the boys a new word. "Do you know what these are called when they're grouped together?" I asked. "They're condiments."

Later that week, my younger son's teacher told me she was interested to hear that we'd introduced him so early to the facts of life, although he seemed to have got a bit confused. He'd apparently sidled up to the dinner lady and said, very secretively: "I know what condoms are," adding later: "... you put salt in them."

I was driving a whole boiling of kids home from school – my own two children and three of the neighbours' – when Luke, my son's best friend, asked me: "What's an orgy?"

I told them about Roman orgies where everybody ate too much, and described the Vomitorium, thinking that would shut Luke up.

Not so. When I'd finished, he grinned at me and said: "That's not why my brother said. He said it's an orgy of sh*gging."

I got into an argument with another motorist while driving my children to school. Windows were wound down and heated words exchanged.

When we arrived in the playground, my daughter ran straight up to some other mothers and told them: "Mummy got really cross with a man on the way here. She knew who he was... he was called 'Wanker'."

Linda Duberley, TV reporter

Miranda aged three had just started nursery school and had the most lovely teacher called Mrs Forsythe. Miranda could not get her tongue round this name and regularly called her something else:

Mrs Four Thighs, Mrs Four Ties, Mrs Four Flies, Mrs Sore Eyes, Mrs Four Eyes, Mrs Four Guys until finally she came out with Mrs Sore Thighs.

I gave up apologising after that.

Daryl Stevenson, children's author and illustrator

I was a form rep in my son's class, and when his teacher invited us to a pantomime she was directing and appearing in with her church group, I decided to take along some of her pupils.

It was typical amateur dramatic stuff - not at all what the six-year-olds were expecting from a pantomime. The microphones didn't work properly, scenery fell over and it was dreadfully long. Afterwards, I had to agree with the boys' verdict on it.

When we got to the car, I realised we'd left Jack's sweatshirt behind, so we traipsed back to the church hall - and bumped into his teacher. We had a chat and I thanked her for asking us to the performance, saying what fun it had been. "But Mum," Jack contradicted. "You said it was really boring!"

My daughter Kitty Dimbleby (now a journalist) has always had a quick wit, sharp tongue and naughty disposition, and I have so many stories about her - which is why she became the inspiration for the heroine of my popular series of 'Kitty' books.

In 1991 she became a pupil (just for two years) at St Paul's Girls' School in London. Many were the afternoons her mouth turned down at the corners when I collected her. Kitty didn't really like school.

The first parents' evening came and I did the rounds of all her teachers, hearing again and again the old 'needs to work harder' line. At the end of her address in the imposing hall, the highly effective and rather daunting Headmistress had announced that she would be in her study if any parents had specific problems or questions.

I had neither but wanted to meet her. No - I wanted to suck up to her. Needed her to be aware of my daughter. So I waited with some others outside the closed door, and at last my turn came.

I sailed in, shook her hand - and began one of those garrulous gushes you blush to remember: "No, no problems... far from it... just HAD to meet you to tell you how very happy Kitty is... adores school... loves everything... smarm... gush... smarm..."

I finished, my face a rictus. There was a pause. Then the headmistress's reply came - crisp, dry and chilly as the first frost. "Oh really? That's not what she told me this afternoon."

Bel Mooney, novelist, journalist and broadcaster

My husband and I had gone along to our daughter's London day school to watch her perform in the end of year play.

During the interval we all filed out for refreshments, and my husband found himself walking alongside a woman who looked familiar. Engaging her in conversation, he asked whether she had also come to watch her daughter.

"No," she replied. "I'm the Headmistress."

A teacher thought we should see an essay our six-year-old son, Rory, had written on the subject of 'My House'. "At home," wrote Rory, "we have a dog, three cats, a goldfish and two naked Mrs Thatchers."

I had made two seven feet high sculptures of Margaret Thatcher, one as the unadorned Venus and the other as Michelangelo's David rising from the waves. They had stood for many weeks in our hallway, awaiting collection for a TV show.

This was all part of normal life in our household for Rory.

Gerald Scarfe, artist

One Saturday afternoon when I was five, my Mum and Dad took me to the local pub. We sat outside and ever the show-off, I soon had the crowd eating out of my hand by singing and tap-dancing on the table. A sweet old lady, with my mother's permission, pressed a sixpence into my hand.

It wasn't until the next Parents Evening that my mum saw my news book entry for the Monday after my 'concert': "I like it when Mum and Dad take me to the pub and I can sing for people to give me money."

I sometimes wonder if primary school teachers choose for public consumption those children's stories that will cause maximum embarrassment to their parents. I came to dread the arrival of the school magazine.

In one issue, one of my sons wrote that his mother was always asleep when he came in from school (I'd fallen asleep once, listening to the radio with my feet up after a particularly busy few days).

Another entry gave the impression that our daughter's bedroom was overrun with mice.

We went to an open evening at our daughter's school, where teachers had made a huge effort to show off the girls' work on desks, tables and around the walls.

We were delighted to find our daughter's story, entitled 'My Daddy', prominently displayed... until we read her observation that: "My Mummy and Daddy are always arguing."

Our young daughter had to compose sentences to show that she knew the meaning of given words. To illustrate her understanding of the word 'hoarse' she wrote: "Mummy and Daddy fight until they are hoarse."

What must her teacher think of us? It would make it even worse if I tried to explain that in reality I never even raise my voice.

I went to a parent/teacher consultation one evening and was just about to say: "Well, of course you hear a lot about us and we hear a certain amount about you - shall we call it quits?" But before I could get the words out, the teacher said: "...and I gather your husband likes to fart loudly in the bath!"

Quiet Please!

© Peter James Field 2006

I was once called out on an emergency job in Washington DC whilst working as a correspondent there. I had to do a live inject from the White House, but I had no babysitter and my partner was away, so I had to take Leila, then aged two, with me.

Half way through the exchange, a little word "Dadda" emitted from somewhere below the camera's view.

At the end of my transmission the cameraman panned down to reveal a small blonde child holding her father's hand. The face said it all... we were fifteen seconds from some serious tears of confusion.

Jon Snow, Channel 4 News presenter

On one occasion, when I was political editor of the Daily Mirror, I had a child care crisis and was obliged to take my two-year-old daughter to an important press conference being given by Neil Kinnock, who was leader of the Labour Party at the time.

I took the requisite notes as I clutched the toddler in my arms at the back of the hall, seeking not to draw attention to myself in any way. When I had heard all that I needed to know for my journalistic purposes that day, I decided to slip discreetly out of the door.

Unfortunately, I had not allowed for the fact that my child was well acquainted with Neil Kinnock, and had no intention of not registering her departure. "Bye bye Neil!" she yelled lustily at the very top of her voice, bringing the entire press conference to a halt. "Byee! We're going now. Bye Neil! Byeee!"

Julia Langdon, writer and broadcaster

It was June 1976. My sister was singing in our school's end-of-year concert being held in the Chapel for parents, staff and pupils. Wanting a recording of the concert, she had given our father her portable tape recorder with instructions to press 'Record' at the appropriate moment.

The moment arrived. The Director of Music lifted his baton and you could hear a pin drop in the packed Chapel. My father pressed the button. Unfortunately, he pressed 'Play', not 'Record'. Into the silence trilled the voice of my sister singing the 1970s hit: *Hey fatty bum bum, Sweet sugar dumpling, Hey fatty bum bum, Let me tell you something.*

My sister's toe-curling embarrassment lasted until our father, fumbling with the unfamiliar buttons, managed to press 'Stop'. The concert never got recorded.

I took my seven-year-old son Sam to see a hearing specialist, as he had glue ear. Sam was getting bored and decided he'd amuse himself by coming behind my chair and trying to pull me up off it by my pants, which were showing just above my hipster trousers. I ignored this; the consultant couldn't see what was happening and we carried on our conversation.

Sam decided to up the ante, so he grabbed my pants, walked backwards as far as he could and then let go of them. The loud 'thwang' of my knicker elastic was like a gunshot in the room and impossible to ignore.

Fortunately the consultant had a sense of humour and we both had a good laugh about it. But my sense of humour was then stretched to its limit when Sam asked very loudly why I was wearing grey pants. "It's called Calvin Klein, darling," I told him.

Fiona Bruce, BBC newsreader

We were in a 'nice' coffee shop in Canterbury, meeting an ex-nanny to catch up on news and in a way, I suspect, for her to check that I was still bringing up the children as she thought fit.

Edward, aged eight, asked in a loud voice: "Mummy, what does prostituted mean?" There was a unified intake of breath and the entire coffee shop fell silent. All eyes swivelled to our table as people waited to see how I'd get out of this. The ex-nanny was stunned.

I decided to play for time rather than launch straight in with an answer, so I said it was a funny sort of word and the meaning rather depended on how it had been used. I asked where he'd come across it. His reply:

"When I went for a walk yesterday, I saw a sign. It said in big letters TRESPASSERS WILL BE PROSTITUTED."

It was someone else's red face that led to our most embarrassing moment. We were staying at a lovely hotel in Rye with our two year old daughter. As is often the case in this country, breakfast was conducted in almost deathly silence.

Sitting at another table were a couple of ladies, one of whom had an unfortunate complexion because of some kind of skin complaint. Suddenly Anna piped up in a crystal clear little voice: "Mummy, why has that lady over there got a red spotty face?"

Thankfully for all of us, we were leaving that day.

Our little girls came to a rather grand wedding with us and loved the flowers and dresses at the church. We then followed the bride and groom in a carriage to the elaborate reception, where we were seated round the Great Hall.

Champagne flowed and we came to the loyal toast and speeches - but my daughter managed to get her bit in first. As we rose to drink to the Queen, a clear little voice echoed through the hall: "Sit down Daddy! You haven't finished your cake."

When my daughter was heading towards her First Holy Communion, so was aged about six, she was chosen to help with the offertory procession. Rather trustingly, they gave her the wine to carry, in an earthenware jug.

Having carried it carefully all the way along the very long aisle, her tongue on her lip with concentration, she handed it over at the altar. Then she belted back down the aisle yelling - and I mean yelling, so the whole enormous congregation could hear: "Mum! There's beer in that mug."

We were taking our young son to Mass, and to make it sound more exciting, I told him we were going to visit Baby Jesus at Baby Jesus's house.

We made our way to the front pew to get a good view. The church was packed and totally quiet. As the tall and somewhat rotund priest walked up to the altar, I noticed Mark looking rather perplexed. Then he said, in a very loud voice: "Baby Jesus is a big chap, isn't he Mummy."

I looked around, hoping that not too many people had heard him, to find stifled laughter coming from most of the congregation. Several people came up to me afterwards and said he had made their day.

A friend of mine was at a prayer meeting, attended by about 20 people. She had taken along her three-year-old daughter, who wandered around the room quietly as people prayed.

At one stage there was a lull in the prayers. Helena was leaning against the vicar (a very proper man in his 50s whom Helena was very fond of). In a very clear voice she announced into the silence: "My Mummy has beautiful nipples."

My friend was so mortified that she grabbed Helena and left - very red faced.

The Things
They Say

© Daryl Stevenson 2006

Ben, aged five, asked why Gertie had suddenly changed from a home-loving dog to a creature that could not WAIT to escape from the confines of the house and garden. Why was she whizzing out of the front door the minute it opened and running away?

So I explained. "Well," I said, "Gertie has decided she'd like to have some puppies, so she wants to go out and find a mate so that she can get together with him and have babies. You know, it's a bit like those wildlife programmes we watch on the television when, for example, a male lion and a female lion get together and then eventually they give birth to some cubs."

I waffled on. Ben listened closely, thought for a moment and then whispered to me (so the dog couldn't hear): "But Mummy, I don't think Gertie's watched any of those programmes."

Daryl Stevenson, children's author and illustrator

We took our four-year-old son to lunch with some friends, who were rather sticklers for good manners. I was keen that he shouldn't show us up, and had impressed on him in advance that he mustn't forget to say 'please' and 'thank you'.

The pudding was delicious - so yummy that when our son was offered more, his manners went right out of the window.

"What do you say?" I prompted him. Still no joy, so our hostess added: "You know the magic word." Indeed he did - and back it came: "Abracadabra."

My son, Tom, was having tea at a friend's house. His friend's mother was valiantly trying to get him to eat his carrots, using all her persuasive powers.

Finally, having had no success, she said: "C'mon Tom, if you eat your carrots you'll be able to see in the dark." To which Tom replied: "I don't need to see in the dark, I've got a nightlight."

Sarah was a very engaging child, full of questions, totally honest and not afraid of chatting to grown-ups. This made her a frequent source of mild embarrassment although her charm usually allowed her, and fortunately us, to get away with it.

Two questions particularly stick in my mind:

To my wife's aunt, an interesting looking woman with a particularly hooked nose: "Auntie Jean - why do you look like a witch?"

And to the vendors of a house we wanted to buy: "...and when we've bought this house from you, what are you going to do with all that money?"

We were in Devon with some Aussie friends when, driving down a hill, we had an altercation with another driver coming up the slope. My Aussie friend, Ben, gave him the full blast of his very best Sydney invective and, somewhat embarrassed, we motored on.

The very next day we encountered an almost identical incident, only this time it was Nick, aged eight, who wound down the window and shouted abuse at the offending driver.

When I asked him why he'd done that, he pointed out that Ben had done the same thing the day before. "But Ben is under pressure," I explained. "He's trying to stop smoking." "I'm under pressure," said Nick. "I'm trying to stop picking my nose!"

John Stapleton, GMTV presenter

In the early 1960s, after a weekly food shop in Cambridge, we treated our toddler to an orange squash at Petty Cury before taking the bus home.

It was also a refuge for rubicund old codgers who sat and yarned over their pints. Snatches of conversation drifted across in ripe Fenland accents. "How are yer, Jimma?" "Not too chipper. If you'd seen me this marnin' struggling with me boots you'd a said 'Poor old sod'!" Our little-un, at an age when new words are quickly picked up, appeared not to have heard.

The bus, as usual at that time of day, was quite busy, but we managed to squeeze onto the long bench-seat just inside the doorway. An elderly gentleman, heavily burdened, struggled past and sank into a seat with visible relief. An anxious little countenance watched him sympathetically. "Poor old sod!" she said.

I was preparing for a concert, and the pianist accompanying me came over to our rented cottage near Haselmere to rehearse, and afterwards to have tea with us. He was a very hirsute gentleman, with a red beard and side whiskers.

All through tea our five-year-old daughter, Rosie, was gazing at him. She was always a very subtle child and after a while, she simply said: "Mummy, I think I've got a lion in my picture book."

The pianist smiled at her and said: "I know, Rosie. I look a bit like a lion." They were firm friends after that.

Ian Wallace OBE, retired singer and actor

When he was little more than a toddler, Louis devised a game to amuse himself at the weekends when all his older siblings were around. He took a black rubbish sack and set about 'burgling' one or two items from each of their rooms, much to their annoyance. After some time, he would re-appear in the kitchen with his 'swag bag', grudgingly returning possessions to their owners after much bartering had taken place.

On one of these days, he returned to the kitchen looking worried. He told us that something was missing from *his* room.

"Perhaps you've been burgled?" I suggested. "Oh no", he replied, "I'm still here, aren't I?"

When my father died, our children were six, eight and ten. We invited them to attend the funeral, but they declined, preferring to go to the church afterwards and be shown where people had sat and where Grandpa was buried.

We were standing by the newly-filled grave when our youngest, Katie, asked in a loud voice, which seemed to carry to the whole village: "If Grandpa is going to heaven, why have they buried him in the ground? It would be much easier for him if they'd put his coffin up in those trees over there."

My mother-in-law had always told us that she would like her ashes to be scattered from a particular spot overlooking the sea on the Pembrokeshire coast.

When she died, her youngest grandson was still at nursery school, and on the Friday before we were due to make this solemn journey, his teacher asked the children what they were going do at the weekend.

She was rather taken aback when Jonathan told her: "We're going to throw Granny over a cliff."

My daughter was babysitting for a four-year-old and her baby brother. One day, their parents wanted to put up some shelves in their bedroom, so my daughter took the children to the park.

The four-year-old got chatting to a man who was there with his child. "Livvy's taking us to the park today," she informed him. "Really?" said the man. "Is Mummy at home, then?"

"Yes," she said. "Mummy and Daddy are banging in the bedroom."

My sister-in-law was in a tea shop with her then four-year-old daughter, Katy. They'd had a nice day out and Katy was in a particularly happy and vociferous mood.

She pointed to a lady and said in a loud voice: "That lady has a pretty hat." The lady looked quite pleased... even more so when Katy followed up her remark with: "That lady has a pretty dress."

Not quite so happy, though, when Katy reached a crescendo with: "She has poopy drawers."

I was shopping one day with my youngest (then aged five or six). We were by the car door, when an old lady walked past and looked down at the little mite.

"Are you helping Daddy with the shopping?" she enquired. "Yes," said my youngest, who then did a 'glass and wrist' shake, reminiscent of the late Eric Morecambe. "And then we're going down the pub."

My mum was looking after a friend's three-year-old son. On the way to the shops, the car broke down and a passer-by stopped to help.

Having fiddled with a few bits, he stood up and said with resolve: "It looks well broken to me, luv." The little lad looked cross, tapped him on the leg and admonished him. "No silly! It's f***ing broke."

Mothers

(Some Children Do Have 'em)

©Judith Brenner 2006

My son had an important football match, and although I'd remembered to put his kit through the wash, I'd forgotten to hang it out to dry. The only thing for it was a quick blast in the tumble drier, along with the rest of the load.

About ten minutes into the match, I could see that he was distracted by something emerging from the short sleeve of his nylon football shirt. The static electricity had obviously attracted something else in the tumble drier - something black and lacy, people noticed, as he pulled it out from his sleeve.

He ran over to where I was watching and, with a withering look, handed me back my knickers.

My 14-year-old son was playing tennis in an away match against a famous public school, and I was on my way to watch. From there, I had to go straight on to a party, so I had made a special effort with my hair.

As I drove up to the school, I spotted my son walking down the road with some of his friends. I called his name and waved hello, and was slightly hurt when he did not even acknowledge me, let alone wave back.

The reason for this snub became apparent when I checked my appearance before getting out of the car - and discovered that I had left one large curler in my fringe.

My mum was chatting with a neighbour over the garden fence. I ran up and started tapping her on the leg, saying: "Mummy, Mummy, please Mummy," with real urgency.

She studiously ignored me for a minute then, apologising to the neighbour for my rudeness, she turned to me and said firmly: "I've told you never to interrupt adults while they're speaking. Now wait till we've finished."

"But Mummy..." "No, you do not interrupt me when I am speaking unless the house is on fire."

"But Mummy..." "Oh for goodness sake, what is it child?" getting really angry now.

"Mummy, the house is on fire." It was too.

I'd promised to be at the school gates at 3.30 prompt to pick up my 14-year-old daughter and some friends for a tennis lesson. Leaving BBC Broadcasting House at three, I was cutting it a bit fine. Had I time to go to the ladies? No. She'd never forgive me if I was late.

I got straight into my car and headed for North London. I made good time and got to the school with five minutes to spare. I jigged around at the school gate, but my bladder had had enough of being ignored.

Fifty or sixty yards away was a leafy cut-through to a neighbouring street, flanked by a few trees and bushes. I looked at my watch. There was just time if I hurried.

I picked an abundant-looking shrub, glanced around furtively to make sure I was unobserved, then dived behind it. Relief at last, fast and furious.

I pulled up my trousers. Something wet touched my ankle. In my haste, my aim had left a little to be desired - the right leg of my light beige trousers was soaking wet above the hem. How to explain that on a bright sunny day? I could hardly say I'd stepped in a puddle. What had happened was only too obvious.

Embarrassing one's children even mildly is an unpardonable sin, but my daughter would be mortified for life if her friends saw me in this condition. I made a dash for the car and called her on the mobile to say I was waiting for her there.

She piled into my old Saab with three of her friends and I just prayed none of them would glance down towards the footwell as I accelerated soggily away.

Sue Cook, BBC presenter

The Metro Centre in Gateshead was the setting for my first experience of a full-blown toddler tantrum and an episode which, thankfully, my twin daughters were too young to remember.

One of the girls launched herself from the double buggy and lay on the floor screaming, arms and legs flailing. On the spur of the moment I decided to do the same to show her what she looked like - to the amazement of the other shoppers.

Some said I was brave; others clearly thought I was completely barking. But it stopped the tantrum - I've never seen a child get into a buggy so quickly. Needless to say, the girls never had another tantrum in public.

I used to set up fun/sexy scenarios for my partner - until one backfired on my two teenage daughters.

One Sunday evening I was working on a really tarty bedroom scene including, for decoration, a black lace bra hanging from a chandelier. It was dusk and I had not yet drawn the curtains.

Although I could not be seen from outside, the decorations could - to the mortification of the girls, when they trooped up the drive with their Church Youth Group, to host coffee.

Afterwards, their language was polite but succinct.

If we'd known about 'that scene', we wouldn't have dreamt of sitting down, with my elderly parents in the room, to watch *When Harry Met Sally*.

As Meg Ryan started, my husband and I sat in embarrassed silence. My father looked up from his newspaper and asked: "What on earth's that terrible noise?" To which my mother replied, without a hint of irony: "I think she's in pain."

My mother was one of those people who talked a lot and tended to speak out before engaging her brain. When I was a teenager our family went on a coach trip, and occupied the back seat of the coach.

On the way home it was beginning to get dark and a little chilly, so the driver switched on the heating system. My mother instantly and loudly exclaimed: "Joanna, has your heat come on?"

When I was about nine, my mother was entertaining a couple of guys from the arts world, who were clearly homosexual. We were all sitting round the dining table and she was talking about a gay time we'd all been having.

She then suddenly put her hand up to her mouth and said: "Oh dear! Maggie told me never to use the word 'gay' these days."

My mother had five brothers, and they treated her as an honorary boy. Their parents were strict about language and the children were well-spoken. However, the boys picked up some startling slang when they went to boarding school (only used out of earshot of adults) and Mother picked it up from them.

She wasn't always clear about the true meaning of the words, some of which she continued to use all her life, dismissing any attempt to put her straight. So after a long session of gardening, she would happily tell any passer-by who admired her handywork that she had enjoyed it but was 'absolutely wanked'.

Mother lived on into her nineties, still occasionally surprising her family and friends, guests, neighbours, the postman, the vicar...

My husband was driving my elderly parents to Salisbury and stopped en route for a pub lunch. My mother is very hard of hearing and my father would talk to her extremely loudly. In the pub, their voices soared above the busy chatter of the Sunday lunchtime clientele.

After the main course, my father went to the Gents. On his return he announced in a stentorian voice: "Well, I've seen everything now - strawberry and cream flavoured condoms!" Silence descended on the pub.

"No, I don't think I want any, thank you," my mother replied. "I couldn't manage anything more!"

A Final Thought

(from actress and comedienne Dilly Keane)

I learned the futility of embarrassment from my mother. Not because she was impervious to embarrassment, but because she lived in constant dread of what I might do or say next.

As a child, she called me by a nickname I hated so much that I can't bear to mention it here, and I still shudder when I hear it. I was teased by schoolmates within an inch of breakdown over this horrible and mortifying nickname, and so I begged her again and again not to call me by that name when we were out, but hers was a heart unmoved by tears or pleading. She would stand at the school gate and call it out in her imperious and carrying voice, freshly salting the wound of my childish embarrassment.

Thus began a war of attrition which became more enjoyable as the years went by.

I was always letting her down. One day when I was about ten years old, some very dull people came to lunch who she had known in her youth. Her father had lived the life of a rich Edwardian gentleman, and so to prove that she still lived in the opulent style that she had known in his house, the preparations were enormous.

The silver was fetched from the bank, the glassware was polished with vinegar and newspaper, and the house was generally overhauled till it sparkled like Bleinheim. Consommé was cleared, lobsters boiled, fatted calves killed, charlottes russed - Escoffier would have been proud.

I got home from school for lunch promptly at

one o'clock. The dining room glittered like Harrods at Christmas. My eyes were popping out of my head.

"Ooh," I said as I lifted my soup spoon, "this is heavy! Where did this come from?"

"We always use these," said my mother crisply.

"No we don't!" I cried, outraged at the barefaced lie. "Our soup spoons are much lighter, and they're a completely different shape. We don't use these either," I added, looking at the rest of the cutlery. My mother ignored me.

A second course arrived. "Coo!" said I. "Two courses! Why are we having two courses?" Then of course pudding arrived. "Pudding? We never have pudding at lunch!" And so it went on. My mother was mortified and I got it in the neck later.

In later years, she trembled behind closed curtains (her words) at what I would write or say next. The successes I had with Fascinating Aida were of course a source of pride, but the pride was heavily outweighed by shame.

This was very good for box office, as I was informed by the manager of the Theatre Royal, Portsmouth, where my parents lived. We were booked in to do a gig there, and when my mother went to church the Sunday after our posters went up, fellow parishioners said they'd seen that we were on. Whereupon she would say very earnestly: "Oh, don't go! It's obscene!"

The following Monday morning there was a queue around the block entirely made up of worshippers from St. Swithun's, and by the end of the day we had sold out.

She came, of course. I gave her the best seats in the house, and she didn't laugh once.

If revenge is a dish best served cold, our relationship was a running buffet at which we took it in turns to bring new and ever more elaborate confections.
But it taught me that embarrassment was the most futile feeling in the world, and to be smiled through at all costs.

CHASE has to raise £3.2 million every year from general charitable donation. Sales of this delightful little book will provide a welcome boost to our fundraising, and we extend our grateful thanks to Frances Coverdale and her sister Clare Price for their dedication and time in compiling these Red Face Stories.

To find out more about CHASE, visit the website at www.chasecare.org.uk.

If you would like to make a donation, please call CHASE head office on 01483 454213.

Bridget Turner, CHASE Director of Care